I0142569

DUET

Lisa Nicoll

Copyright © 2020 by Lisa Nicoll

All rights reserved. This book or any portion thereof may not be reproduced or used in any manner whatsoever without the express written permission of the author except for the use of brief quotations in a book review or scholarly journal.

First Printing: 2020

Cover image and design by Lisa Nicoll
Book design by Maxim Jones

ISBN: 978-0-578-74306-6 (paperback)
ISBN: 978-0-578-76489-4 (ebook)

Tree House Atlantic
New York & United Kingdom

www.lisanicoll.com
inquiries@lisanicoll.com

CONTENTS

DUET

Holy sites,
divinity school,
sacred texts.

As if
everything
isn't already.

I

ALPHA

After heavy snow,
one wolf cuts a path through,
leaving prints the others
step into.

The wind doesn't bite them
inside the narrow confines
of the packed walls
plowed by his shoulders.

Each paw deepens the print,
and the way is clearer
for the next in line.

May we be
efficient and thoughtful
as wolves.

DISCERNMENT

Like someone raised in a culture
with a thousand words for snow,
don't rush in claiming to know
which one it is this time.
Arrive there as it falls,
and land together.

COORDINATED EFFORT

With rest in my bones
like nutrition, my muscles
raise me and we walk,

even in the dark,
even to places I fear
I do not belong,

and what happens is
something like force, something like
tenderness shepherds

me and my muscles
and my bones to the edge of
was and will be now,

and because I am
clearly not alone, I am
able to proceed.

WHEN YOU ARRIVE

Whether you've traveled
a block or an ocean,
you'll have changed
where you stand
in space and time,
catch-all terms for
an infinity of coordinates,
for when and where you arrive,
stop, and consider Orion's belt head-on.

[When you think]

When you think
you don't matter,

please instead
allow yourself

to be thought,
(and by)
a better god.

WINGS

I've learned something about wings.
It's simple. I'll bet children know it.

If you see a butterfly working hard
to shed a chrysalis, nearly there,
stand down.
Do not help the butterfly.
If you do, you will kill it.

In its struggle to escape
what once was cozy,
it builds muscles
and becomes itself.
Nature's perfect timing.

I'm in terrible pain.
Do not help me.

(I am calling myself a butterfly,
a monumentally dumb move
which could move anyone reading
to such embarrassment—
for me, for themselves,
for butterflies—

they'll (you'll) feel it
nearly impossible
to resist the urge to save
me from myself.)
But please

do not help me.
I want to live.

[Like a first dream in a second language]

Like a first dream in a second language

or a phrase of music just sketched,

like something
there isn't a word for in English,

you extend your hand
and we shake.

GETTING WARMER

I have
accepted
a challenge.

Everything
until now
has been
my approach
to the ascent.

Well-prepared,
I lack for nothing but

the certitude of climbers
who know
their anchor has integrity,
but the mountain has more.

SPAN

What if angels were red?
What if they ripped heads off prey
and this was mercy?

What if their cry,
that piercing alarm,
is the song of songs we long to hear,
announcing deliverance?

What if they could hear across
not only great distances,
but also planes, and epochs,
into a thought
that causes one heart
to beat faster.

What if their purity is this:
Annihilation. or: Nothing.
Hunger. or: Deliverance
of fools
they do not suffer.

SIGHTED

I remember being
friends with the air.
I used to play with air.

I remember falling
to my death on Earth.
I used to fear all death.

I remember being
nested by the push,
surprised by what I knew:

that we were the weightless things,
with unbreakable anatomy,
and will and sight like God.

I LEARNED TO SPELL G_D

I learned to spell G_d
this way, with an underscore
where the o should be.

The idea was that that
which is G_d
is unnamable,
that we sully by even trying,
that to name is to diminish.

All our names for everything
in all our languages,
especially secret ones
between children and twins—

all the vowels,
all the consonants,
all the sounds they make,
alone and combined,
all the shapes they make,
by architect or calligrapher,

spell what we're talking about:
the underscored space.

(There's a kind of intimacy that is far-flung)

When I encounter
a secret part of myself
in someone's work,

my breath catches
for a second that splits
like an atom wiping out

any sense of being separate.

TRANSISTOR

It is 1982.
I am aware I am alive
and have a vehicle
to take me places quickly—
places like the fire pond,
your neighborhood,
and the underground stream.

The transistor radio
in the basket of my bicycle
is tuned to nothing in particular,

because what I'm into is that stretchy tone
between stations, and all I'm saying is
it doesn't NOT sound like a recording
of whales I found in the basement in one
of my dad's old *National Geographics*
when I was down there playing
records from before I was even born.

GOOD NEWS

If when we are young
those we are entrusted to
compromise, break, or
leave, that is the thing
we bond to and are bound to
break open ourselves.

BIRCHWOOD

Inside a silver forest is the neighborhood
I grew up in. It still bends
into a pale canopy over wild
blackberries growing within reach
of children encountering first upon first.

II

INCLINATION

At the top of a Ferris wheel
overlooking a waving black
sea sit two children swaying
in the seat, about to turn

thirteen, about to
for the very first time

taste spun sugar
at the fingertips
of the other—

they just know
they were made for it,
they've been waiting
their whole lives
for this moment,

and when a gust comes
and swings them,

each lets go of the painted bar
and becomes instead
what the wind holds onto.

I MAY LEAVE

I may leave in the middle
of a movie, or a storm, or the night

if that's when one of us first acts
as if the other isn't important.

I DON'T KNOW WHAT TO CALL YOU

You are no ordinary feather.

You sprang from the chest of an accipiter
slaloming through pine groves at speed,
here to increase, here to challenge
all current conditioning in your
weightless, unbreakable form.

I can see you from where I stand
calculating exponents, adjusting
with precision, responding
to a single quiver

that is the barrier giving way
until—*boom*—you're through
and through something
no one saw coming
or knows what to call.

TURNSTILE (HOW TO MAKE AN ENTRANCE)

I watched a young woman walk through a turnstile,
exiting Grand Central Station. At the threshold
but definitely through—the mechanism clicked
a revolution—she paused and tapped the toe of her boot
behind her heel—first one, then the other—
as if to shake off snow or dirt
before entering the house.

(It was a dry, sunny day.)

Her movement, absentminded and ingrained
as the Sign of the Cross or a subject's curtsy,
was how this young woman learned to enter spaces,
was how she stepped into the cathedral
of her day.

TOTAL LUNAR ECLIPSE, SUPER BLOOD MOON
(20 JAN 2019)

From the roof of my building,
what was clear was that I was
staring down the bisected
vein of a god.

(All that happened
was the Earth interrupted
a conversation between
the Sun and the Moon.)

LAVA

I don't know my great-grandmother's surname
because it was misspelled so many times.

I know her married name, but not her own,
not what her friends called her as a girl
when they asked if she could come play
and their mothers asked which Caterina.

All the cleavings have come to roost in me.
I am a tangle of fissures, of names misheard
to suit a chillier climate.

One spelling I've come across is *Stramandinoli.*
One is lava. One is great. One is blood.

ANIMA

Like any animal
who's just escaped
with her life after
a very long run,

paralyzed,
I shake out.

PASSAGGIO

If you had asked me yesterday,
I'd have said no, it's not possible
to hear something shouted
into the packed yellow earth
of Sicily over and over
a hundred years ago
now, but now
I've slept on it,
yes, of course, yes
I can hear
the shouting, sanguine
and clear as glass,
yes, of course, yes
I can feel
the island shifting in its seas
as its children left:
I am their eventuality
shouting back.

CONCH

I.

The human ear picks up sounds
made by the human body:
blood flowing, muscles acting,
which the human brain will
normally discard.

When louder, external sounds
are filtered out, however,
these subtler constants
roar.

The occlusion effect.

II.

Hold it in your hand.
Feel its proper weight.
Raise it to your ear.

Listen to someone
rushing with blood,
action, and the sea.

QUIET

This is a new vast.
This room is live.
I can hear plants
grow and insects
cross ceilings.

I can hear you.
I can hear blood.
I can hear Earth's
rotation in my sleep.

[After I've been to the sea]

After I've been to the sea,
I feel clean because I am, because,
without thinking, I've been thought.

FOURTEEN

I met and fell in love for the very first time
   on Cape Cod
with a boy who lived there year round
and was a wicked swimmer.

He was the best friend
of my best friend's boyfriend,
they all had beach jobs,
and he liked me, too.

All we seemed to do and wanted to do
was roll around in the sand and feel
every inch of each other's body
and our own.

When we'd had enough of that,
there was the ocean.

We got hot at the same time.
This was my favorite thing.

   Oh my God it's so hot we have to go in—
   Oh my God yes—

and he'd pull me by the hand
up off the blanket
and we'd run laughing down the beach
straight into the icy Atlantic

where sometimes we'd lose each other's hand
    for a minute,
but then a wave would deposit us
onto each other's shocked new body

in the extraordinary relief of love.

(This letter is for you)

Dear ____,

I hope this finds you well,
refreshed by the ocean,
resting in easy anticipation of
what happy work lies ahead.

Although you and I know
each other hardly at all,
I felt compelled to write
a few words tonight
that have fallen
into my lap from
the sky we share,
and seem, somehow, to be
addressed to you.
(Any excuse.)

Here you are:

      You're not imagining things.

(I mean that in the gentlest sense.
The tone is "Yes, you're 100% right
about what you're feeling. You're
not lying to yourself to get by.
You got it. That's exactly right.")

A more accurate way to say it might be:

> What you're imagining is true.
> The other party is imagining
> the same thing, and probably
> isn't sleeping right now, either.

Anyway, that's it. Thanks very much for reading, get some sleep, and welcome home.

In all sincerity,

Lisa

III

[At night something travels]

At night something travels

silent as an owl's flight
through a forest,

covering a great distance
and closing it

when it lands
on the same branch
inside different people.

ALCHEMY

Your work

fills
my lungs

with air.

MURMURATION

If you want
to go somewhere else,
go there.

Meet someone
who's having the same idea
you are, at the same time.

Starlings do this
and we can see
how beautiful it is.

THE LIKES OF YOU

I've gone off wine
since encountering
the likes of you.

Dry, racy, lean;
earthy, full, crisp;
you rise up and
introduce yourself with hints

of citrus, but beside a fire
inside a very warm lodge
made entirely of glass and birch,
surrounded by snow so soft
people call it powder

and debate its color
as the sun sets
and they sip.

IT'S NO WONDER YOU DOUBT

A mendicant without an order,
you hardly recognize the feeling
in your chest right now
and are afraid
it's a condition
come to kill you.

Not all monks subsisted on scraps
as their soles wore down;
some illuminated manuscripts
with strokes of real gold,
and drank ale
with every meal.

Find a mirror and recognize yourself.
The you in the poem
is you.

[The space that you occupy]

The space that you occupy inside my chest
is a prism of stained glass and sunlight,
arches and spires.

The floors are slate and heart pine
worn smooth by striding Franciscans.

There is a chalice for each of us
of cool water the mystics talk about.

The bells that ring on the hour
include us in their reverberations;
in solo and unison, we chime back.

And just outside, an ocean full of salt
will hold us up like an offering to the sky,
should we decide we want to go in.

SEPTEMBER

Go mad with grief and lust.
Mourn even the dying of grief.

Love someone so completely
you're left in shock when they go

and don't take you with them,
and grief takes you

into the next world,
where all you want is

to love
with abandon again,

even though.

FIRST SNOW

Like children
run to a window
at first snow,

rise
to the occasion
of each other.

THIS IS A PHOTOGRAPH OF THE SUN
(I SOMETIMES FORGET OUR SUN IS A STAR)

Waves move through a star's interior
because of changes in temperature.

Heat rises from the core of the star
to its surface, where it cools and falls

back down inside and this movement, this
up and down motion of heat, creates

waves that leap around inside the star
(did you have Spirograph?) and jostle

its surface constantly—like jello,
we'd say, if we could see properly,

or like an altar boy on the rope
of a cathedral bell, ringing.

(Fig 1a. The sun rings the figure like a bell.)

DUET

I.

Will you love me
when I am old?

People will have
stopped noticing me.

II.

[

            ]

I.

[

            ]

II.

I remember
when you died

in my arms and well
into your future.

I.

[

                    ]

II.

[

                    ]

I + II.

Inside the open
heart is certainty.

We count time here
in measures.

I.

[

II.

                    ]

THESE DAYS

When I say thank you,
what I mean is:

You are the lantern
Virgil holds.

IV

ACTUALITY

As long as we don't
mistake the walls and floor
for reality, we'll wake up

in an entirely new place
after every nap and night.

FOUNDLING

If one day you find yourself
in an unfamiliar part of the woods
behind your house, look for the wall
crawling with ivy and crumbling.
Close your eyes and feel for the chain.
This will be where, if you push,
the immovable door will give.
An isosceles too narrow for anyone
but you will appear. Go on.
Rooms containing quantities
impossible to measure
wait.

DRAGONS

Be able to say
to the people back home:

I went over the horizon line
into a city of dragons.

They swallowed me whole
and in parts, and taught me how.

They are more terrible than you fear,
made, as they are, of your refusals,

and they love absolutely. They breathe it.

Who do you think turned me around
and pinned this note to my chest?

Who do you think signed
the names of the archangels?

[When I became this creature requiring care]

When I became this creature requiring care,
    I panicked and howled.

What did you do when you perceived the distance
    you'd come to navigate,

denied even a primitive tool like daring
    to comprehend the source of thunder?

THE OBSTETRICIAN

welcomes us in when
we first arrive, wet and shocked
we're breathing at all,

one constellation
delivering another
into a new sky.

ALLOWED

1. You are
   totally allowed
   to change
   your mind.

2. I am
   totally allowed
   to change
   my mind.

3. We are totally allowed
   to change our minds.

4. Totally means totally.
   Totally means no exception,
   in all circumstances,
   even when
   people get mad.

[The part of you that is eternal]

The part of you that is eternal,

that you or they have tried to reduce
to an occasional sneaking suspicion,

is what is called for.

UNDER OUR PALMS

Whenever we meet,
you come running.

At first, you'd stop short
of where I was by at least a meter.
Once, you came all the way to the door
but then didn't come in,
despite holding flowers
(maybe because).

Last night, though,
we sat together on the curb.
No one ran anywhere.
We just sort of arrived here,
hugged our knees to our chests,
and rested our chins.
You asked me if I wanted a piece of gum
and I said OK.

It's grape, you said.
I love grape.

That settled, we stretched
our arms behind us and leaned back.
Our legs flopped to the ground
into mirroring fours and you even said
Four as I was thinking it.
Totally, I said, and blew a bubble (purple).

The gravel was so uncomfortable
under our palms
we had to keep adjusting
and saying things like OW
and oh my God what is up with this street
and inching and showing
each other the concrete
embedded in our upturned hands.

COURAGE

I'm afraid I'm far
less brave than I imagined
I'd be, now I'm here.

LOVE

Fear it as it approaches. Fear it as you and an other near its yielding border and are surprised by its easy pull and clear welcome. Fear it as creatures feared the first eclipse. Fear it as the sentient fear the monumental. This is origin. This is all the gods. This is the stag and the fawn and the doe.

This is gentle.

PHOENIX

You defied a giant to be here.
You lowered the bridge
without waking the dogs;
you charmed guards
and crossed the length
of the great hall
in under a minute.
When you passed
his open bedroom door,
he stirred
and progress halted,
and you were grateful
for the time
saved in the hall.
At his exhale,
you took advantage
of the wind,
and continued
to the staircase
you came to descend.

Now at the molten core,
you dive in without a splash,
and, from limbs to fins to feathers,
ascend.

SHELTER

In the center of the woods
in the valley of the park
on the path that swells between
two waterfalls
and, in winter, has sheltered
courting owls,
I rest.

V

ORCHIDS

Someone I know once
picked up a mirror leaning
on my bedroom wall

and flipped it around
in a burst of decision
when he saw himself

in it, in full-length,
and didn't like what he saw.
He then turned back to

me, replaced his hands
on my shoulders, and resumed
the kiss we were in.

I don't know what he
saw that he didn't like, but
I didn't see him

again after that,
and I found him beautiful
and unusual.

In each of us lies
the worry we'll be revealed
as unfit for love.

I later learned he
cultivates orchids, those rare,
exacting creatures.

SURNAME

Ironed and fastened with a pin
   or used to wipe up and knotted;

all your fathers' sides
   (containing all your mothers');

you are its furthest point,
   and your children after you.

You are the forebear now
   of sash or gag.

HOLOGRAM

When I remove my contact
lenses,

the world appears
as I see it.

RED

There are certain reds
I am oxygenated
by seeing even
a splash of. Yours are
like this, like Claret in a
chalice being raised
to human lips, or
the spray at the outskirts
of a far nebula.

PAINT ME

Use bones and branches and hair
from animals without language
you understand;

use your teeth and other blades
to crush lapis and roots into
pigments that approximate
what happens when I travel
across a great room and you

filter that distance through
the color of your eyes.

LIFT

Your name
how it travels
down my spine
like an impulse
remaining from
when we were birds.

MAYBE YOU'RE READING THIS

When icy snow strikes the glass
like scattershot in the dead of night
and wakes me, do you know my
first thought after checking the
usual spots for leaks is of you?
From what I can tell, you don't
know. You don't seem like someone
who knows someone inside thinks of him.
If I'm right, I wonder how
to let you know I've checked for
leaks and there are none, my home is dry,
my bed is soft, everything is warm,
and I'm up. I wonder how
to let you know I've written this down
for you and me both. I don't
mean to be cryptic, it's just
how you send me, not like scattershot
but showers of shooting stars.

[I woke from a dream of herons]

I woke from a dream of herons
and the shadows they cast

to your soft dark hair
lifting and falling
against my skin
with each
oscillation
of the fan.

Sleeping beside you,
I grow intimate
with the strength
of feathers.

WAY OF LOOKING

Women! Look at the body
your grandmother gave you and thank her
for sharing her proportions.

Take a photo of yourself
and slide it under the frame of a
mirror you look in often.

Affix it at eye level
or higher. Look up to it, like you
would look as a little girl.

RECENTLY I'VE LEARNED

Recently I've learned someone loves me.
It's quite a thing, when that person is kind.

Recently I've heard someone hates me.
That's quite a thing, too, regardless.

Recently I've played villain and beloved
in two stories at once, and believed them both,

just because I was in them (starring, even)
which feels like power, which is quite a thing.

MAXIM

I will always love you. If
you love me or not, or love someone
else. These are the conditions

I find myself in. These are
the conditions I used to pity
in other people.

May everyone love like this.
Unrequited, unconditional,
absolutely, regardless.

LET

Have you let it break your heart?
I don't mean in two. I mean shattered.
I mean into pieces like
dust only smaller. I mean
split like the God particle like proof
of it like something we need
a microscope to see.

FOLDING

Today I washed linens.

Today I reached back
into things we said
to each other, mostly
to shake out the sheet
now that it's dry
and fold it
with my hands
in a way I hadn't.

This is a form of praying.

[Because you are extraordinary to me]

Because you are extraordinary to me,
I look for you everywhere,
even in mirrors.

I know they burned your body,
but I'm talking about
what remains present.

VI

FLUENCY

Now that you have emerged
resigned to no fate,

now that you have relieved
all phantoms of their duties,

loose your ribbon,
unweave your braid,

assume your seat
beside the generals:

your sentinels are loyal
and sharp as hawks,

and there's work to be done
in at least two languages.

CRUSHED

From a place of absolute terror,
I pull off my shoes and leap
into a vat of blood red grapes.
My ankle winces and I slip
but right myself with the next stomp,
knowing full well this is the way
to make wine.

EVOLUTION

Inside
the body is
a timer set to nothing
recognizable,
designed to refine us.

Unless your life
is almost
over in one way
or another,
it doesn't flinch.

Think of
the prey animal
who lives.
Think of how far
she has brought
Gazelle.

SNAPSHOT

This is a long one.

You don't have to read it.

It's only a snapshot,

but it's hurtling
through space.

WITHOUT TITLE

*I don't even know what to call this, it's so common. It should
be uncommon. It should be unheard of. It should be done,
once and for all, and never again, to anyone.*

When I was twenty,
I worked for a doctor who raped me.
I had rent to pay, so, after blacking out,
returned to work, where he smiled at me
like someone I could trust, and I had
my first seizure.

The doctor was a famous man
women lined up for, I was told.
He was fifty years my senior,
so I in no way understood why
women wanted to turn his head
clean off.

This is why today,
what I write about is love
and the sacred sovereignty of space.

This is why today,
what I photograph is beauty
and the infinite gift of my own body.

GOOD COMPANY (YOU ARE HERE)

You are here.
Immaculate and vast
as a molecule,
as easily overlooked
or missed.

FEBRUARY, VERY EARLY

Later, when someone finds
your imprint in the snow,
they'll probably stop
and wonder if
you're a hunter, or if
you came this far in the cold
for the ice itself,
to see
what you could hear.

[Yesterday afternoon I changed]

Yesterday afternoon I changed
my room around entirely.

The bed now faces in a direction
it never has before,

and last night my hair,
damp from a late shower,
dried in waves

from a breeze
that could finally reach me.

WILL

I.

Once upon a time, I chose
confidants who sold my secrets
and nearsighted, trickable guards.

II.

A close relation has died.
In a room lined with carvings,
counsel hands me an envelope,
sweaty, as if he had ridden days
to reach me without letting it go.
Inside is a large key.
I take possession.

III.

A kingdom whose architects
positioned it over and around
a source washers and seers alike attend
is now my privilege to protect.

IV.

I swallow the key
and smooth out the envelope
before secreting it inside
a massive tome
in a once living language.

SHED

There will come a day when you think
oh I couldn't possibly, but then you do
and nothing breaks but the doubting
to reveal to you the obvious muscle
of your human heart.

ADJUSTING TO THE LIGHT

When cathedral doors twice my height
close behind me
and I'm inside,
blind as a newborn,

I am ecstatic.

When a hemstitched cowl breaks at the shoulder
and drapes across the back of a Benedictine
and I see it,
plain as linen,

I am ecstatic,

as ecstatic as I am now,
recalling folds
to myself, to you,
to someone who is reading.

ADMIT ONE

Careful consideration
deposits me here, where I am now
someone I'm not at odds with.
This is the ride I came for.
What exhilaration, saying so
for the first time, stepping through
the gate gripping a tail
of tickets damp from my hand
and the sea, counting off
the right number, watching
the barker's hands as he tears
the seam, gives me back the rest,
and like that, I'm admitted.

LUPINE

When I look in the mirror
not like a heat-seeking missile but
plainly, it's my grandmother

I see, relaxed as a wolf
surveying the landscape, gaze softened
but including everything.

Lisa Nicoll is a writer and multidisciplinary artist whose work involves the liminal and the belief that all space is sacred. Her dramatic work and musical compositions have been performed at The York Theatre, Backstage at 54 Below, and the Oxford Playhouse (UK). Her poetry and fiction have appeared in journals including *The Metropolitan Review,* and her visual art is in private collections in the US and UK. She is a member of the Dramatists Guild and lives in Brooklyn.

lisanicoll.com
@lisa.k.nicoll
inquiries@lisanicoll.com

www.ingramcontent.com/pod-product-compliance
Lightning Source LLC
LaVergne TN
LVHW041231080426
835508LV00011B/1154

* 9 7 8 0 5 7 8 7 4 3 0 6 6 *